An opinionated guide to

EDINBURGH

Written by
PIPPA PERRIAM

National Galleries Scotland (no.7)

INFORMATION IS DEAD. LONG LIVE OPINION.

When we conceived these guidebooks, we feared they would fail. Who needs a guidebook when everything can be found online for free?

But then it occurred to us: that's exactly why you *do* want a guidebook. You want lively, trustworthy opinion combined with great photographs. You don't want endless information from a thousand online bots.

We think you are like us: you care about quality, you care about style, you care about provenance, but you don't have time to waste on long words like 'provenance'. You want to cut to the chase: where's good?

We are an independent from London. How dare we write a book about Edinburgh? Because we work with passionate local writers who seek out the spots that remind us of the east London we know and love: these are the most creative, diverse and exciting places of all.

Ann & Martin, co-founders
Hoxton Mini Press

The view from the walk up Arthur's Seat (no.45)

Sotto (no.28)

Opposite: Water of Leith (no.48)

EDINBURGH
MERCANTILE
THE NEW CURIOSITY SHOP
HOMEWARE + GIFTS
Beautiful Objects
LUXURY ITEMS
18
OPEN

Lannan Bakery (no.31)

Opposite: Edinburgh Mercantile (no.37)

BEYOND THE FRINGE

It's easy to come to Edinburgh and only scrape the surface. That's not a criticism – it's a consequence of just how good the famous things are. Edinburgh Castle (no.5), rising from ancient volcanic rock above the Old Town, really is one of the most dramatic sights in Europe. The Edinburgh Festival Fringe (no.4), which kicks off every August, is the largest arts festival on the planet. It doubles the city's population and transforms pubs, church halls and at least one broom cupboard into venues that are, for a moment, the centre of the cultural world.

But these icons are just the most visible products of something that has always run deeper here. Edinburgh has long been a city of ambition and invention: this is the place that sat at the heart of the Scottish Enlightenment, that revolutionised surgery and published the first modern encyclopaedia, that gave the world the decimal point and the digestive biscuit. But this spirit didn't remain in the history books – it's still very much alive, still creating, still moving things forward. And you can find it beyond the usual tourist hotspots.

Leith, which was a separate town until the 1920s, has one of the most exciting dining scenes in the UK. Still a working port, it now also has restaurants like Dogstar (no.26) and Ardfern (no.25) that have earned it a reputation that extends well beyond the city.

In Stockbridge, that same energy shows up differently: this is a neighbourhood that feels like a village has ended up in a city, built around independent businesses that each offer something remarkable, from Golden Hare Books (no.41) to Jorum Studio (no.35) perfumery.

Bruntsfield, Marchmont, the Southside – each neighbourhood carries its own distinct rhythm, its own expression of this restless, creative city. And because Edinburgh is so compact (I always estimate that nowhere is more than 40 minutes on foot), you can spend your morning in one world and afternoon in another.

And then, alongside its urban charm, is nature. For all its architectural drama, shops and restaurants, Edinburgh holds more green space than any other of the UK's most populated cities. The hills are not a backdrop but part of the city: Calton Hill (no.47) and Arthur's Seat (no.45) are just two of the seven peaks within the city limits, offering views that stop people mid-sentence (and that's not just from being out of puff after summiting them). Within 20 minutes of the centre, you can be in the Pentland Hills (no.46), surrounded by lochs and peaks, with Edinburgh entirely out of sight. It's a rare thing: a capital city where the wild feels so close.

This book is an attempt to show you all of it – the city that we, the locals, are so proud to call home. You'll find the restaurants worth crossing the city for, the shops worth taking your time to browse in, the green spaces worth lacing up your boots for. Come for the headline attractions – but fall in love with everything else.

Pippa Perriam
Edinburgh, 2026

ABOUT THE AUTHOR

Pippa Perriam is an Edinburgh local who has spent over a decade exploring and celebrating the city's best independent spots. Her work now spans food, travel, lifestyle and insider guides to Edinburgh and beyond.

ABOUT HOXTON MINI PRESS

Hoxton Mini Press is a small indie publisher based in east London. We make beautiful books with a dedication to sustainable production and great photography. When we started the company, people told us print was dead; we wanted to prove them wrong. Books are no longer just about information, but objects to collect and own.

BEST FOR...

Families

Little ones can run riot around Jupiter Artland (no.6), which has acres of outdoor sculptures, including Charles Jencks' giant landforms *Cells of Life*. There's plenty worthy of adult attention too. The Royal Botanic Garden (no.44) lays on activities throughout the school holidays, while The Free Company (no.24) provides lots of space at its farm-to-table restaurant.

Date night

Spry (no.55) is the perfect spot to share a bottle of natural wine in chic minimalist surroundings. Little Capo (no.23) has a satisfyingly buzzy atmosphere, or go to The Last Word (no.58) if you want somewhere candlelit and seriously sexy. And finally, there's Sotto (no.28) – because what's more romantic than sharing a bowl of freshly made pasta, *Lady and the Tramp*-style?

A rainy day

Dominion Cinema (no.9) is the only place to spend a wet Edinburgh afternoon catching the latest releases in a reclining seat with a glass of champagne. Hours could easily be spent wandering Surgeons' Hall Museums (no.10), or pop to Valvona & Crolla (no.38) to assemble the ingredients of a special dinner you can take your time making while staying cosy indoors.

Breakfast

Head to Norah (no.20) for a frankly life-changing bowl of brown sugar-topped porridge. Ante (no.30) is perfect if you're looking for pastries or a sit-down breakfast. If you're not fettered by tradition, Ardfern (no.25) has an all-day menu that offers you burgers before noon with no judgement (but get the hash browns too).

A quick lunch

Hand-ripped noodle specialists Pomelo (no.16) offer a short but consistently incredible menu for fast decision-making. Alby's (no.22) giant focaccia sandwiches are fuel for even the busiest days. Mother India's Cafe (no.21) is central, moves fast and feeds well – making it the go-to between Fringe shows in August.

Seasonal cooking

Scotland's produce shines at The Palmerston (no.19), an unfussy but refined bistro, while Dogstar (no.26) really comes into its own during game season (from August to February). At Montrose (no.27), foraged ingredients make for a menu that shifts with the land as much as the season.

On a budget

The set lunch at Stockbridge Eating House (no.15) is one of the best-value meals in the city. National Galleries Scotland's (no.7) permanent collections are completely free – don't miss Dalí's lobster phone in Modern One. Enjoy a night out for under a tenner catching a work-in-progress comedy night downstairs at The Gilded Saloon (no.17).

A PERFECT WEEKEND

FRIDAY EVENING

Check into Gleneagles Townhouse (no.51), centrally placed for exploring the city. Hop on the tram outside and travel just two stops for dinner at The Palmerston (no.19). Afterwards, head to Hey Palu (no.57) on Bread Street for the best Negronis in town.

SATURDAY MORNING

Join the queue at Lannan Bakery (no.31) on Hamilton Place – it's worth the wait. Then cross the road to Fortitude Coffee (no.13) to caffeinate, before setting off along the Water of Leith (no.48). Follow the river to Dean Village, passing by the neoclassical St Bernard's Well.

SATURDAY AFTERNOON

Retrace your steps back to Stockbridge, and you'll be just around the corner from Stockbridge Eating House (no.15), where you'll knock elbows with neighbours enjoying a set menu that punches well above its price point. While on St Stephen Street, make the most of its independent shops. Pop into treen (no.33) for clothing with a conscience, or Jorum Studio (no.35) for unique fragrances. From there, a lazy loop around the Royal Botanic Garden (no.44) is the perfect way to walk off lunch.

SATURDAY EVENING

Snag a reservation at Little Capo (no.23) on Howe Street, or take your chances on the walk-in bar seats – arguably the best in the house. This small-plates spot with an Italian flavour is one of the hardest bookings in the city for good reason.

SUNDAY MORNING

A short walk from the hotel, Calton Hill (no.47) is the city's best viewpoint – panoramic in every direction. The monuments are good to wander round, including the notoriously half-finished National Monument. Head down to Ante (no.30) on Haddington Place for coffee and an interesting breakfast.

SUNDAY AFTERNOON

Venture out to organic farm The Free Company (no.24). Take a seat at long communal tables, and make sure to order their own reared beef, the star of the Sunday roast menu. After, head to the Mound and spend an hour or two at the National Gallery (no.7). Marvel at European works from the Renaissance through to the early modern period, alongside a beautifully renovated Scottish Gallery. The rotating exhibition programme means there's usually something new to catch.

SUNDAY EVENING

End the weekend at the Port of Leith Distillery (no.11). The top-floor bar offers sweeping views across Leith harbour, the Firth of Forth and Edinburgh city. Then head around the corner to Dogstar (no.26) for dinner – one of Leith's most sought-after bookings.

1
AN ARTY RIVERSIDE WANDER

Begin at the National Galleries Scotland: Modern ❼ (there are two side-by-side galleries, Modern One and Modern Two), where you can pick up the Water of Leith path (beside the Modern Two gallery). The river will guide you from here – follow it and let the city gradually build up as you head into town. The first stretch takes you through the sheltered tranquillity of Dean Village, before the path opens out into bustling Stockbridge. Grab a takeaway from Fortitude Coffee ⓭ if you need refuelling, then carry on along the river to St Mark's Park, keeping an eye on the water – not only can you commonly spot wildlife like herons and otters, but Antony Gormley's *6 TIMES* standing figures also appear at intervals through the river. The path ends at The Shore in Leith, where Barry Fish ⓮ is perfectly placed for lunch or an early dinner. Finish the afternoon at Port of Leith Distillery ⓫. Take the tour or simply head straight to the top-floor bar to soak up views over the docks with a cocktail in hand.

Length: 7.6 km

Walking time without stops: 1–2 hours

Start: National Galleries Scotland: Modern

6 TIMES (Figure VI)
11
LINDSAY RD
14
FERRY RD
GRANTON RD
6 TIMES (Figure V)
LEITH WALK
St Mark's Park
6 TIMES (Figure IV)
INVERLEITH ROW
EAST FETTES AVE
LONDON RD
13
6 TIMES (Figure III)
QUEEN ST
CANONGATE
Modern One
Modern Two
COWGATE
7
6 TIMES (Figure I)
6 TIMES (Figure II)
500m
1km
1.5km
N

2
INDIE SHOP-HOPPING IN STOCKBRIDGE

Start at Lannan Bakery ❸❶ on Hamilton Place. Arrive early enough to have your pick – a pastry or two for now, and perhaps something for later. From there, pop along to grow urban ❹❸, a haven for the green-fingered, before wandering along onto St Stephen Street, one of Edinburgh's best independent stretches: browse the rails at treen ❸❸, pick up a fragrance at Jorum Studio ❸❺ and poke around the shelves at Edinburgh Mercantile ❸❼, where you'll inevitably find something you didn't know you needed. Skout ❸❷ sits just down the hill, where you can rummage for vintage furnishings and accessories, and from here it's a short walk to the Royal Botanic Garden ❹❹, its lawns providing an ideal picnic spot. The glasshouses are worth a look too, particularly in winter, when the warmth hugs you at the door. Loop back down through Inverleith Park for lunch at Sotto ❷❽, settling in for pasta and Italian red wine, then finish the afternoon at Smith & Gertrude ❺❹ around the corner, where one glass has a habit of becoming several.

Length: 3.4 km

Walking time without stops: 30 minutes–1 hour

Start: Lannan Bakery

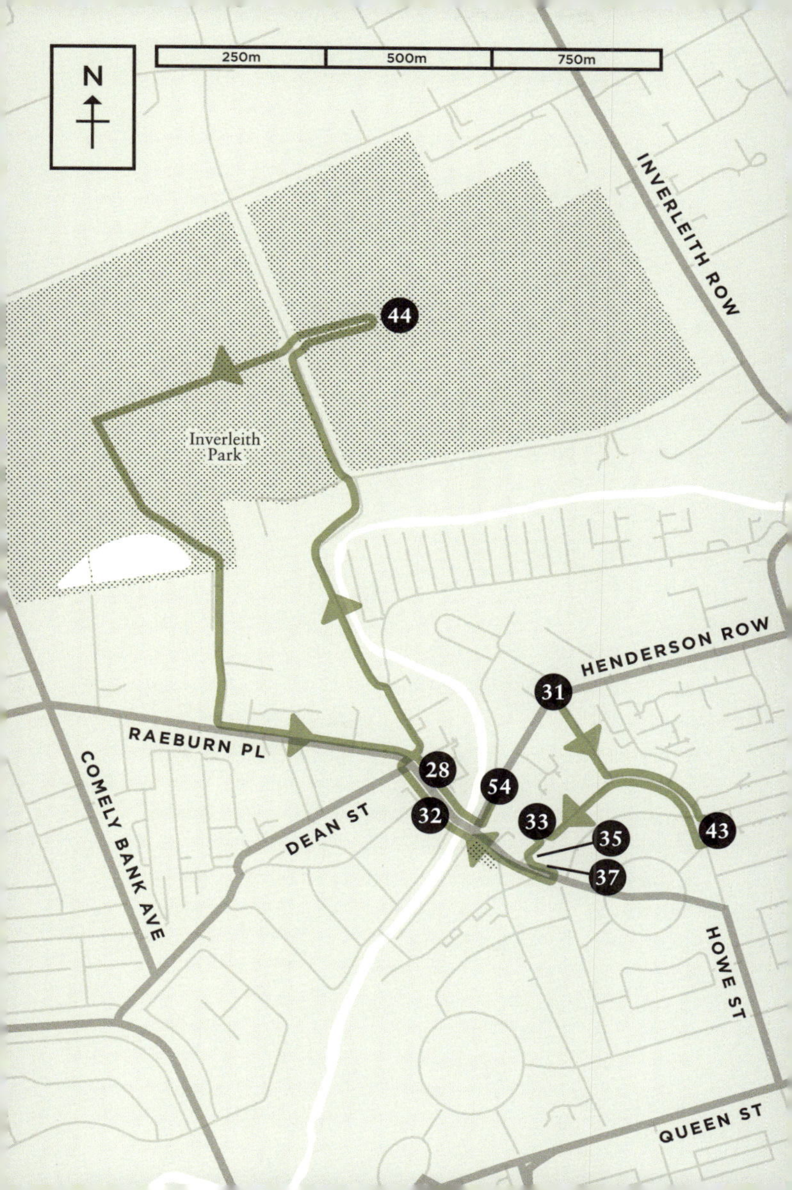
N
250m
500m
750m
INVERLEITH ROW
Inverleith Park
HENDERSON ROW
RAEBURN PL
COMELY BANK AVE
DEAN ST
HOWE ST
QUEEN ST
44
31
28
54
32
33
35
37
43

3

CLIMB THREE OF EDINBURGH'S SEVEN HILLS

Start at the Fruitmarket gallery (8), right beside Waverley Station: stop in for a coffee and a bite to eat at the cafe, take in whatever's currently showing (the programme consistently pulls in major names) and browse the bookshop before you set off. From there, cross Waverley Bridge and head east along Princes Street and up onto Calton Hill (47) for the first of the day's panoramas. The climb takes minutes, but the views are spectacular, with the whole city laid out before you. Go back down and through the Old Town, working your way up the Royal Mile to Edinburgh Castle (5). You don't need to go in to make it worthwhile – the Esplanade alone offers another great vista. Then head south through the Grassmarket and up Candlemaker Row to Sandy Bell's (53) on Forrest Road for a half-time pint and, more likely than not, some live folk music. Fortified, cross The Meadows and make for Arthur's Seat (45) – the full summit takes around an hour at a steady pace, and the views from the top make Calton Hill look like a warm-up act. Descend south towards Newington and reward yourself at Pomelo (16), where the hand-ripped noodles and chilli oil are exactly what tired legs deserve.

Length: 9.3 km

Walking time without stops: 1.5–3 hours

Start: Fruitmarket

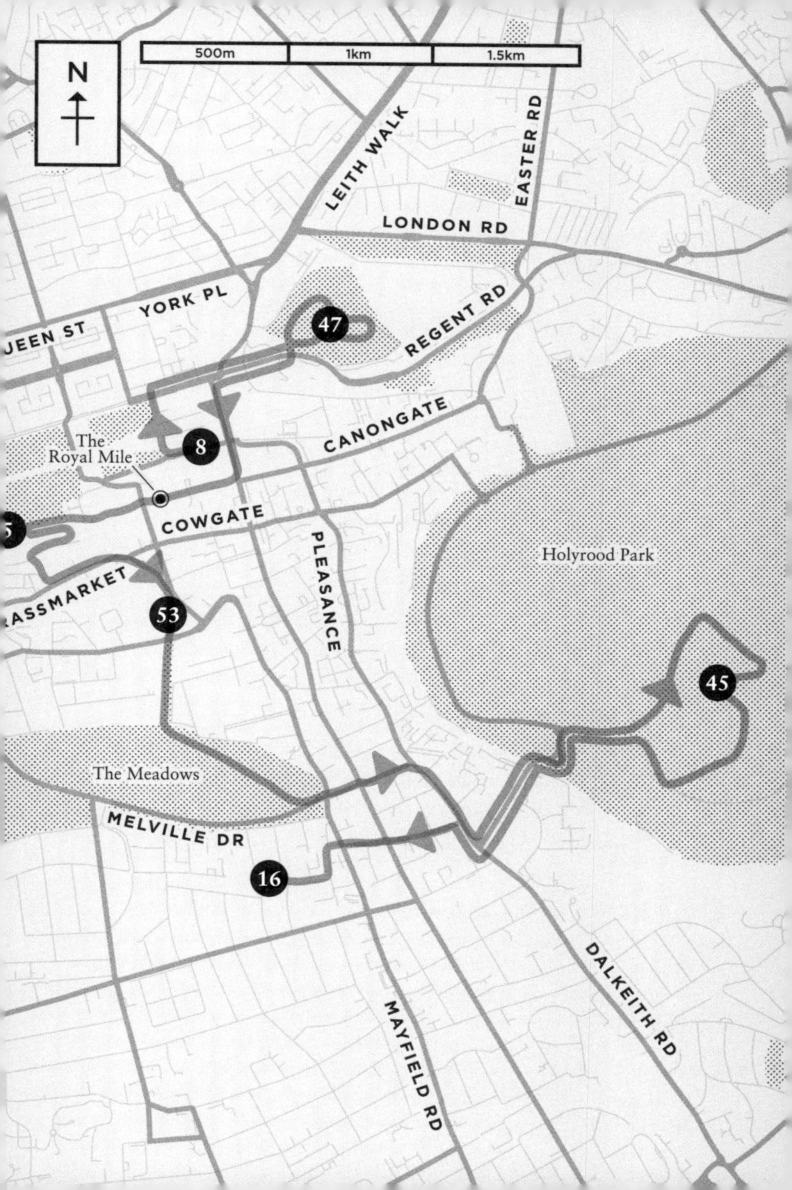
N
500m
1km
1.5km
LEITH WALK
EASTER RD
LONDON RD
YORK PL
JEEN ST
REGENT RD
47
CANONGATE
8
The Royal Mile
COWGATE
5
ASSMARKET
53
PLEASANCE
Holyrood Park
45
The Meadows
MELVILLE DR
16
DALKEITH RD
MAYFIELD RD

4

THE EDINBURGH FESTIVAL FRINGE

The world's biggest performing arts festival

The Fringe will overwhelm you if you let it. Every August, thousands of street performers take over the city, with comedy, dance, music, theatre and everything in between filling hundreds of venues right across town. The mistake a lot of people make is packing their days too tightly. My tip is to leave room to be surprised and delighted: pass a venue and scan its board for the shows pulling good reviews, and when a flyer distributor collars you, hear them out – you might be richly rewarded (or not, which is equally in the spirit of things). You'll want a base to regroup too. Mine is George Square Gardens, where food trucks ring the edges and there's plenty of space to sit down with a pint before diving back in.

Various locations, check website for details

edfringe.com

BEST
40
www.edinburghart.com
20

5

EDINBURGH CASTLE

The city's fortress in the clouds

An icon of the city, Edinburgh Castle is impossible to miss, perched high on an ancient volcanic rock above the Old Town. You'll spot it peeking out across the skyline from almost every vantage point – and you might hear it too. At 1pm each day, the One O'Clock Gun fires, often catching unsuspecting passers-by on Princes Street off guard. If you have time, it's worth heading inside to explore one of Europe's oldest fortified sites, with highlights including the Scottish Crown Jewels and St Margaret's Chapel, the earliest surviving building in Edinburgh. If not, walk up to the Esplanade for free, where sweeping views and the castle's imposing facade still make the climb worthwhile.

The Esplanade, Castlehill, EH1 2NG

edinburghcastle.scot

6

JUPITER ARTLAND

A sculpture park to get lost in

Ever fancied taking a swim in a sculpture? Here you can do just that: Joana Vasconcelos' *Gateway*, an immersive artwork that doubles as a fully functioning swimming pool, is part of the 30-strong permanent collection at this art estate, just a 25-minute drive from Edinburgh. Sculptures are scattered across 120 acres of meadow, woodland and gallery spaces, with works by Tracey Emin, Anish Kapoor and Antony Gormley appearing as if from nowhere as you wander the trails. And because this is truly an art land, even the cafe is a feast for the eyes, the walls decorated in an immersive, surreal mural by artist Nicolas Party.

Bonnington House, The Steadings, Wilkieston, EH27 8BY

jupiterartland.org

7

NATIONAL GALLERIES SCOTLAND

Old masters and modern icons

Got five minutes to spare, or five hours to lose? Scotland's national collection is spread across four galleries in the city. The beautifully renovated flagship National Gallery on Princes Street is the easiest starting point, home to European masters and featuring everything from late-Victorian progressives, the Glasgow Boys, to Landseer's *The Monarch of the Glen*. There's a rotating exhibition programme throughout the year, and the (free) Turner in January show is a guaranteed highlight. Modern One and Modern Two lean contemporary, while the striking neo-Gothic Portrait Gallery regularly stages excellent photography exhibitions.

National: The Mound, EH2 2EL

Modern: 73 & 75 Belford Road, EH4 3DR

Portrait: 1 Queen Street, EH2 1JD

nationalgalleries.org

THERE WILL BE
NO MIRACLES
HERE

NATIONAL GAL
National
Gallery

8

FRUITMARKET

Central free arts space

Arriving in Edinburgh by train? This should be your first stop to sample the city's vibrant art scene. Right next to Waverley Station, the Fruitmarket is a brilliant, free gallery with a constantly changing schedule of contemporary exhibitions and events. Its programme regularly attracts major names, with artists such as Louise Bourgeois and Andy Goldsworthy having exhibited here. The small bookshop by the entrance alone is worth a browse, packed with art titles and more unusual gifts (a great spot to pick up something for the hard-to-buy-for). There's also a cafe for a quick coffee or bite before heading on, making it an easy, often overlooked addition to even the tightest itinerary.

45 Market Street, EH1 1DF
fruitmarket.co.uk

Upper Gallery
Lower Gallery
EMMA HART A LONG HARD LOOK

9

DOMINION CINEMA

Art Deco cinema glamour

Stepping into the Dominion feels like pulling back the curtain on the golden age of cinema. Nestled down a quiet residential street in Morningside, its bold Art Deco facade appears almost theatrically between the surrounding houses. Inside, this family-run independent shows the latest releases, but it's the glamour that sets it apart. Since long before the big chains caught on, they have been offering table service to your seat (including champagne if you really want to indulge). Seating ranges from armchairs to sofas and recliners, and in some screens you'll even be handed a complimentary tub of Pringles – a small detail, but a rite of passage for many Edinburgh filmgoers in our youth.

18 Newbattle Terrace, EH10 4RT
dominioncinema.co.uk

DOMINION
1234
DOMINION
DC

10

SURGEONS' HALL MUSEUMS

Medical curiosities and surgical history

Walking through rows of preserved body parts in glass jars isn't for everyone – it is, undeniably, a little macabre. But get beyond the initial shock and you'll find one of the most fascinating museums in the city, charting the evolution of surgery in Scotland and Edinburgh's role at the forefront of medical innovation. One of the oldest museums of its kind, with items dating back to the 1600s, the collection spans anatomical specimens, early surgical instruments and more interactive displays that help bring it all to life for both grown-ups and children. You could easily spend hours here, though it's perhaps not the best stop straight after lunch if you're at all squeamish.

Nicolson Street, EH8 9DW

museum.rcsed.ac.uk

11

PORT OF LEITH DISTILLERY

Modern take on Scotland's whisky craft

This is a whisky distillery like no other – a bold claim in a country with over 150 of them. Situated beside the water in the heart of Leith, just a 20-minute tram ride from the city centre, the UK's first vertical distillery rises 40 metres high, stacking the entire whisky-making process floor by floor. Tours take you up through each stage and include a taste of the raw spirit, offering a rare glimpse at whisky in its earliest form: their first barrels won't be ready until 2027, so you're catching something at the very start. Even if whisky isn't your thing, the top-floor bar and restaurant are worth the visit alone, with panoramic views over the docks – the perfect spot for a sundowner.

11 Whisky Quay, EH6 6FH

leithdistillery.com

12

SANTU ROASTERY

Cafe and roastery in Victorian surroundings

Just behind the top of Leith Walk, this cafe and roastery blends serious coffee with serious style. Set in brilliantly unusual surroundings inside a former Victorian washhouse, you'd easily walk past if you didn't know it was there. Venture inside and you're met with the toasty aroma of freshly roasted beans, sourced directly from farmers in Brazil, with the roastery itself just metres behind the counter. Seating is limited, but if you manage to grab a spot, look out for traces of the building's past in the original signage and features. It's perfectly placed to pair with a wander through Leith or nearby Broughton.

23 Union Street, EH1 3LR

santucoffee.com

ANTU COFFEE

SANTU
COFFEE

13

FORTITUDE COFFEE

Edinburgh roastery with Stockbridge outpost

If I'm in need of a caffeine fix while wandering between Stockbridge's independent shops, this is where I'm heading. Fortitude hits that sweet spot of great coffee, easy location and a reliably bustling atmosphere, with a steady stream of locals (often with dogs in tow) popping in for a takeaway. They roast their own beans, so if you like what you're drinking you can pick some up to take home. And if you forget, don't worry – the distinctive bags of beans crop up in cafes and shops across the city. It's also perfectly placed for a takeaway cup before a wander along the nearby Water of Leith (no.48). Their second outpost is only a five-minute walk from the Royal Family's Scottish seat, the Palace of Holyroodhouse, if that's on your itinerary.

66 Hamilton Place, EH3 5AZ
Other location: 4 Abbey Mount, EH8 8EJ
fortitudecoffee.com

14

BARRY FISH

Scottish seafood with a Mediterranean soul

In Scotland, 'barry' means good – as in great, brilliant, excellent. So, when chef Barry Bryson opened his first restaurant, naming it after himself felt only right. It sits on the Shore in Leith, a couple of miles north of the city centre and about 20 minutes by bus or tram, in a stretch of pretty harbourside buildings that can feel more Copenhagen than Edinburgh on a clear day. Fife-born Bryson spent years cooking across Europe, particularly in Spain, and those Mediterranean influences show up in the confident, clean flavours. Now back home, he builds his menu around prime Scottish seafood, letting top-quality fish and shellfish do most of the talking (but offering plenty of choice for non-seafood fans too).

62 Shore, EH6 6RA

barryfish.co.uk

15

STOCKBRIDGE EATING HOUSE

Bijou bistro for an affordable lunch

This is Edinburgh via Le Marais, channelling the spirit of a classic French bistro. Paper toppers protect checked tablecloths from buttery spills and wine rings, and a chalkboard of daily specials is brought to your table. The menu keeps things simple, featuring local fare with a small but perfectly formed wine selection to match. At lunch, the set menu is one of the best-value meals in the city, while dinner calls for the aged marrow and beef burger, served with a gravy boat of sauce au poivre for dunking or drenching. Vegetarian options are limited, but what they do, they do very well (that goes for the Negronis too).

7 St Stephen Street, EH3 5AN
stockbridgeeatinghouse.co.uk

16

POMELO

The best hand-ripped noodles in town

Situated on a quiet residential street, Pomelo might just serve the best noodles in the city. Undeniably, they're the go-to order here – satisfyingly chewy, tangled up with crackly fried pork or vegetables and plenty of chilli oil. They even feature on the brunch menu (noodles for breakfast is no hardship), alongside dangerously addictive garlic chilli hash browns with a salty-spicy topping. Basically, you can close your eyes, point at anything on offer and know you've chosen well. With its small premises, booking ahead is wise, and expect to be dining shoulder-to-shoulder with fellow patrons.

27 Sciennes Road, EH9 1NX
pomelocafe.co.uk

17

THE GILDED SALOON

Neighbourhood pub and comedy venue

A casual pint here can easily become a full night out – without ever having to leave the premises. Upstairs, an inviting pub pours local beers and spirits, including taps from local Leith brewery Newbarns (no.56). Its kitchen, led by award-winning Edinburgh chef Tomás Gormley, turns out some properly good food – expect hearty gastropub classics like pies and Welsh rarebit alongside sharper touches such as dressed crab crumpets. Downstairs, entertainment partner The Gilded Balloon (one of the main venues of the Edinburgh Festival Fringe) keeps the energy high with a rolling programme of comedy and live theatre. Great if you're in a big group.

47 Lothian Street, EH1 1HB
thegildedsaloon.co.uk

18

NISHIKI

Day-to-night Japanese spot

The move here is to arrive in the morning for a Japanese take on a full English – miso-glazed bacon, onsen eggs, shimeji mushrooms, Japanese sausage and toast with nori butter instead of your usual fry-up. If you're after something more traditional, there's a classic set too, with grilled fish, miso soup and pickles. The mostly counter seating, set within a cool concrete interior, makes it an easy win for solo diners. Come later and things shift into a more familiar rhythm: ramen, sashimi and yakitori skewers sit alongside delicious small plates, giving the space an intimate izakaya feel by evening.

151–155 Morrison Street, EH3 8AG
nishikiedinburgh.co.uk

19

THE PALMERSTON

Thriving bistro and bakery

You could describe The Palmerston as nose-to-tail dining, but it's far from clichéd. This is one of Edinburgh's most talked-about restaurants for good reason: confident cooking that's serious about flavour but relaxed in spirit, served in a setting that hums from morning to night. They work closely with local producers, so the menu shifts with the seasons. My favourite seat is at the bar, where conversation flows and the team might just pour something interesting from an off-menu bottle. Whatever you order, begin with hunks of home-made sourdough and salty cultured butter. Visit in the morning and that same bakery supplies pastries, strong coffee and loaves to take home.

1 Palmerston Place, EH12 5AF
thepalmerstonedinburgh.co.uk

NILE

20

NORAH

Daytime dining spot on the water

Norah has an immediate, homely ease about it. Right on the waterfront in Newhaven (just a short walk from the tram stop, roughly a 25-minute ride from the city centre), this butter-yellow cafe is named after the owner's Irish grandmother, and that heritage gently shapes the menu. Chalkboard specials and simple wooden chairs give it warmth without fuss. Soda bread appears in different guises, from breakfast with a boiled egg, Coolea cheese (Ireland's answer to Gouda) and pickles, to ice cream later in the day. The brown sugar and cream-topped porridge is reason enough to make the journey down at breakfast time. No reservations, but weekdays usually mean you'll find a table.

3 Pier Place, EH6 4LP
norahnewhaven.co.uk

ORIGINAL
HP
SAUCE

21
MOTHER INDIA'S CAFE

Buzzing spot for spicy small plates

Everyone in Edinburgh seems to have a story about Mother India's Cafe. A much-loved neighbourhood fixture, it's been the backdrop to countless dining experiences over the years – everything from big, budget-friendly student meals to spirited work nights out. Some would even swear it's the best Indian in town. The menu is built around smaller plates designed for sharing, with a mix of familiar favourites and regional dishes, and plenty of choice across dietary preferences. It's vibrant, unfussy and reliably good. Come August, it's particularly in demand, sitting right in the heart of the Fringe action and offering a dependable, satisfying – and, most importantly, quick – break between shows.

3–5 Infirmary Street, EH1 1LT
motherindia.co.uk

22
ALBY'S

The home of stacked focaccia sandwiches

Your first thought when faced with an Alby's sandwich is usually: how on earth is my jaw meant to get around this? These towering stuffed focaccias are unapologetically huge, packed with bold fillings for both meat-eaters and vegans alike. They've been slinging them out from their Leith base, a 20-minute tram ride from the centre, for years, and now have a smaller Southside spot too (ideal for an alfresco lunch on the nearby Meadows). Expect a regularly changing menu and weekend specials built around big flavours. My trick is to order one to share so there's room for sides – the prawn toast is a standout. You can also order ahead on their website for collection to beat the queues.

8 Portland Place, EH6 6LA
Other location: 94 Buccleuch Street, EH8 9NH
albysleith.co.uk

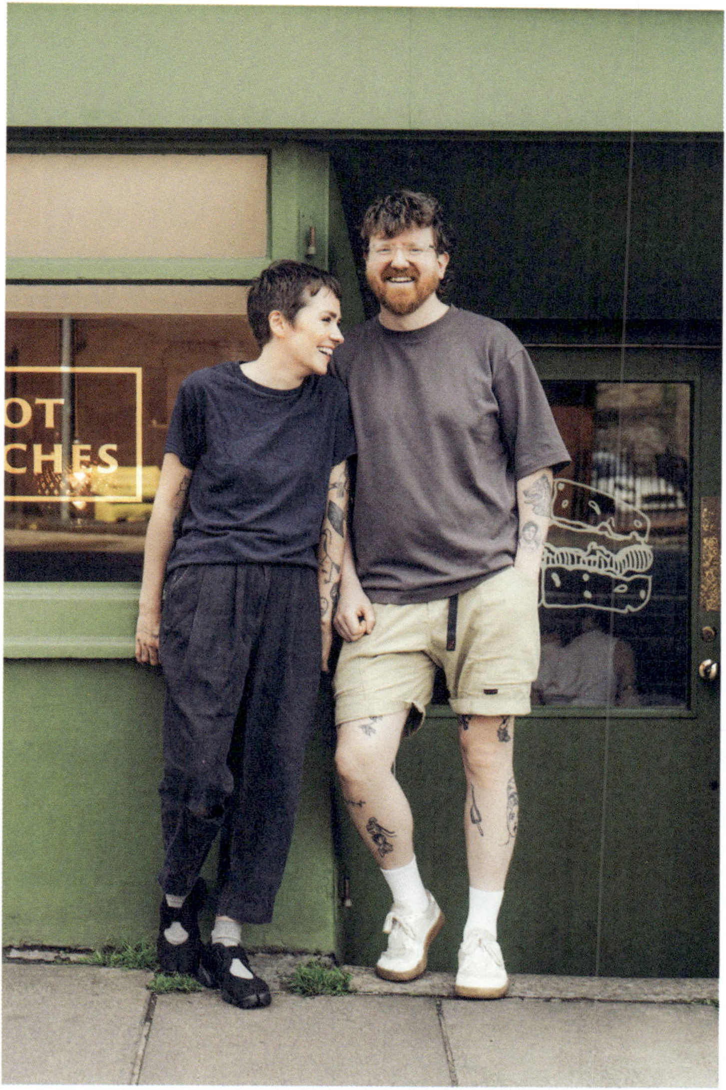

ALBY'S

23

LITTLE CAPO

Italian-ish neighbourhood restaurant

Little Capo in the New Town quickly became a favourite with Edinburgh's restaurant crowd. The menu is built around sumptuous small plates, from burrata with freshly made focaccia to calamari *al vino rosso* – ideal for couples, groups or solo diners. Sitting between the city centre and much-loved Stockbridge, it's one of the hardest reservations to land – bookings go live 30 days out at 9am. Some space is held back for walk-ins, but if you can, aim for the central tiled bar. It's undoubtedly the best seat in the house and the centre of the action.

18 Howe Street, EH3 6TG

littlecapo.com

OWE STREET
little
CAPO

Burrata, Fennel,
Mackerel Crostini,
Zucchine Fritte,
Calamari Fritti,
Salumi,
Heirloom Tomatoes,
Risotto,
Pappardelle,
Caponata,
'Cioppino',
8oz

24

THE FREE COMPANY

Organic farm and dining experience

On arrival, you'll pass rows of beds containing vegetables that will soon be on your plate, before entering a wood smoke-scented courtyard where fellow diners gather around an open fire. Venturing inside, the dining room is housed in a former milking barn, now home to long communal tables where guests enjoy a seasonal, ingredient-led menu. This organic regenerative farm opens for lunch and dinner towards the end of each week, earning a Michelin Green Star in 2026 for its close connection to the land. It's just outside Edinburgh, but the journey is part of the charm – hop on the 44 bus on Princes Street, and you might even be returned in their old Land Rover Defender.

Cockdurno Farmhouse, Balerno, Midlothian, EH14 7HZ

the-free-company.com

25

ARDFERN

All-day feasting done right

Few places in the city have nailed the all-day eatery concept quite like Ardfern. Drop in for brunch, settle in for their raved-about Sunday roast or pull up a seat at the bar for wine and oysters later on – you're in safe hands at any hour. The hash browns are non-negotiable, topped with delectable combinations (creamed corn and black garlic being a recent highlight). Their smash burgers have achieved cult status and regularly pop up at other venues across the city. Enjoyed a wine you sampled? You can take some with you by purchasing from their onsite bottle shop.

10–12 Bonnington Road, EH6 5JD
ardfern.uk

26

DOGSTAR

Snug eatery with a killer drinks list

When a Michelin-starred chef teams up with the brains behind one of Edinburgh's best-loved bars, you can expect something special. Dogstar opened in 2025 and quickly became one of Leith's hottest reservations, with weekend spots snapped up weeks in advance. The drinks list is as sharp as you'd hope, including 'one gulp bangers' designed to kick things off properly. The menu centres on Scottish ingredients, with dishes made for sharing. The room is intimate, so grab a seat at the bar if you can. Keep an eye out for their Jimmy's Fried Chicken pop-ups, a 2020 side project that counts on a devoted following and is still widely considered among the best around.

17 Portland Place, EH6 6LA

dogstarleith.com

DOGSTAR

DOGSTAR

27

MONTROSE

Tranquil wine bar and elevated restaurant

Stepping into this 19th-century former inn feels like entering an immediate oasis of calm. Downstairs, a lively wine bar pours biodynamic bottles from niche European growers, while upstairs the dining room is more muted, with soft light and the faint curl of incense in the air. The food is technically brilliant, with menus that shift regularly, making use of foraged ingredients. You can go all in with the tasting menu, where the kitchen really flexes, or drop in for a more casual set offering at the weekend. Look out for regular events, with visiting winemakers and regional dining takeovers.

1 Montrose Terrace, EH7 5DJ

montroserestaurant.co

Wine list

28

SOTTO

Relaxed Italian dining in Stockbridge

Sotto champions seasonal Italian cooking, with a menu that roams across regions rather than sticking to the usual classics. Head inside and you'll immediately spot the shelves heaving with Italian bottles, all available to drink in or take home. A long communal table brings together a mix of both locals and visitors – from well-to-do Stockbridge characters to friends sharing focaccia and vino – while the compact kitchen hums away in the background. Downstairs offers a more traditional dining room, but the spirit is the same. My tip is to grab a seat at the window – ideal for a glass of wine and a bit of people-watching.

28–32 Deanhaugh Street, EH4 1LY
sottoedinburgh.com

28-32
ENOTECA & TRATTORIA
Sotto
ENOTECA & TRATTORIA

29
LYLA

Seriously chic fine dining

This is Michelin-starred fine dining with a refreshingly relaxed edge. LYLA has all the hallmarks of a classic high-end restaurant – yes, even those neat little stools for your handbag – yet the atmosphere never tips into stuffy. The menu is centred on sustainably sourced fish from the Scottish Isles (the lobster tartlet snack still lives on in my memory years after dining here). The tasting menu experience begins upstairs in the lounge, where you can settle in with an aperitif while watching chefs assemble delicate snacks at the counter. Downstairs, the theatre continues in the main dining room, where an open kitchen offers a front-row seat to the calm choreography of service.

3 Royal Terrace, EH7 5AB
lylaedinburgh.co.uk

30

ANTE

Creative, ever-changing daytime cafe and bakery

Hidden down a short flight of stairs, this small cafe and bakery from the team behind Spry (no.55), punches well above its weight. The menu is constantly changing, which feels refreshing in an age of pre-planned orders and Instagram previews; here, you arrive curious and see what's come out of the kitchen that day. Expect clever twists on familiar breakfast and lunch dishes, like orange posset with pecan granola in place of the usual yoghurt bowl, or a perfectly cooked omelette baveuse served with slices of house-baked bread. Speaking of which, their bakery is worth a visit in its own right, whether you're sitting in or picking up something to take with you for the day ahead.

1b Haddington Place, EH7 4AE

instagram.com/ante_coffee

ANTE
SOURDOUGH £4.2

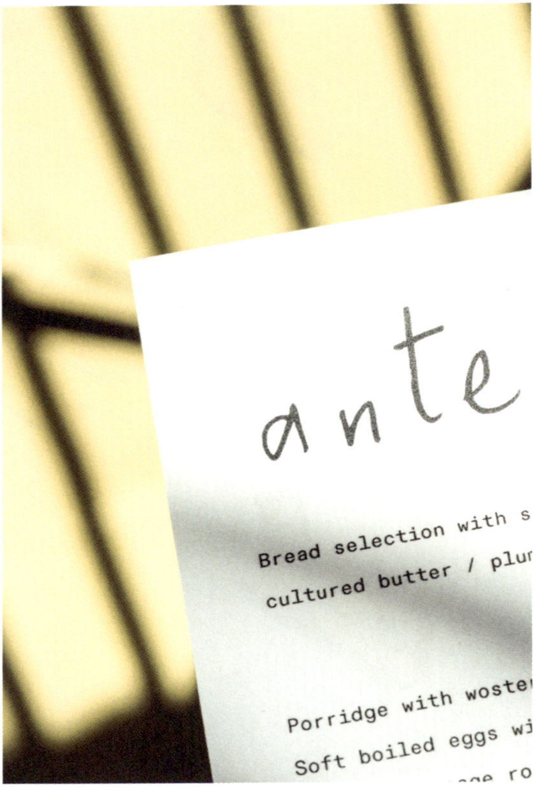
ante
Bread selection with
cultured butter /
Porridge with
Soft boiled eggs

31

LANNAN BAKERY

World-renowned bakery worth the hype

Lannan has become one of Edinburgh's most talked-about bakeries for good reason. In its first year, Darcie Maher's cream-and-crimson shop picked up a prestigious French La Liste award for best new pastry opening – high praise from the home of the croissant. There's almost always a queue, and rightly so: impeccable viennoiserie lamination (buttery layered pastry), beautiful bakes, plus focaccia sandwiches that sell fast next door in their Pantry shop. Crucially, it tastes as good as it looks. Pre-order online and collect from the Pantry to skip the wait entirely, but if you haven't thought that far ahead I'd recommend arriving just after opening time to have your pick of the day's offering.

29–35 Hamilton Place, EH3 5BA
lannanbakery.com

COFERASTA
COFERASTA

32

SKOUT

Perfectly curated crafts and curiosities

If 'coastal grandmother' is your vibe, you'll fall for this little gem of a shop. It's a hodgepodge kind of place where you never know what your rummaging will uncover – which is half the fun, right? The shelves are filled with vintage and second-hand finds, mixed in with small-batch knits and ever-changing accessories: everything from endearing ceramic animal figurines to quaint, hand-painted crockery. And if something catches your eye, grab it – it won't sit around for long. Crafters will be especially happy here, with regular darning workshops and baskets of yarn and needles waiting to be picked through.

45 Deanhaugh Street, EH4 1LR
skoutedinburgh.com

skout
Collectables & Curiosities
45
FOR SALE

33

TREEN

Sustainable fashion retailer

This store, which stocks both men's and women's wear, champions clothing with a conscience, whether that means natural fibres, ethical production or timeless design. A mix of heritage British brands and Scandinavian newcomers creates rails that feel considered rather than trend-led. It's the place you come to invest in pieces you'll still be wearing years from now, with staff who really know their fabrics and fit. Beyond clothing, there's a tightly curated lifestyle selection too, from home fragrances to self-care staples. You'll also find garment care essentials, including eco-friendly clothing washes, to help extend the life of everything you buy.

2–4 St Stephen Place, EH3 5AJ

shoptreen.com

Women
Men
Lifestyle

WATER
METAL
WOOD
AMBER

MIRROR WATER
MIRROR WATER

34

FRONTIERS MAN

Independent menswear boutique

Frontiers Man is for style-savvy men who don't need flashy brand logos to prove it. The store's tightly edited mix of indie global labels includes hard-to-find New York brands. The emphasis is on quality fabrics, clean lines and pieces designed to endure beyond a single season – timeless silhouettes that outlast trends. Footwear is standout here, from well-made sneakers to classic leather work boots. The shop sits opposite its equally sophisticated sister store Frontiers Woman on William Street, a handsome Georgian stretch lined with independent bars and restaurants – perfect for a wander on a spare afternoon.

18 Stafford Street, EH3 7BD

frontiers-man.com

T.REX
ROLLING STONES

35

JORUM STUDIO

Handcrafted perfumes inspired by Scotland

Jorum captures the spirit of Scotland in scent, distilling landscape, weather and memory into fragrances that feel both unexpected and deeply rooted in place. The brainchild of Scottish perfumer Euan McCall, this St Stephen Street studio produces scents that are bold, layered and almost guaranteed to provoke admiring questions (I'm always asked what I'm wearing when it's Pony Boy). The ever-growing range includes the Scottish Odyssey collection, inspired by everything from coastal bonfires to wild moorlands. If you're looking for something that carries the essence of your time here long after you've left, this is where to find it.

12 St Stephen Street, EH3 5AL

jorumstudio.com

SPIRITCASK
PONY BOY
FIREWATER
NEC TAR Y
ASKR
ELEGY

JORUM

36
TBCO

Hip outpost for accessories and home decor

Famed for their colourful triangle scarves and patterned pyjamas, local brand TBCo has earned cult status among the city's fashion crowd for its bold accessories. Entering their Leith showroom, you can browse racks of clothing alongside thoughtfully designed soft furnishings, all sustainably produced under their B Corp credentials. The space doubles as a source of interiors inspiration too, with beautifully styled bedding setups showcasing their textiles. Beware: you can come in for a quick look and leave with a long wishlist. My gifting pick? Their super-soft lambswool blankets, which can be personalised with an embroidered message – go bright and modern or opt for a more classic tartan.

170b Great Junction Street, EH6 5LJ
tbco.com

Coorie
Home

170B
Certified
B
Corporation
tbco.
tbco.
DESIGNED TO MAKE AN IMPACT
tbco.
OPEN

theo.
SLOW
SEASONS
The Art of

37

EDINBURGH MERCANTILE

Covetable homewares and beautiful objects

It's hard to leave Edinburgh Mercantile empty-handed. The carefully curated selection of practical goods has a way of making you realise you needed something all along: who knew your life was missing an elegant broom? It's particularly good for the hard-to-buy-for, with everyday objects elevated to something a little special. There's a subtle vintage utilitarian thread, from soap on a rope to timeless enamelware and durable stainless steel servers. Stationery lovers are well catered for too, with stylish pens, papers and tools that balance function with considered design.

18 North West Circus Place, EH3 6SX
edinburghmercantile.com

38

VALVONA & CROLLA

Edinburgh's premier Italian deli since 1934

If a beautifully wrapped wedge of cheese appears at an Edinburgh dinner party, the inevitable admiring question is, 'Is that from Valvona & Crolla?' Multiple generations of Scottish Italians have built this extraordinary emporium of produce, and stepping inside is a feast for the senses. Floor-to-ceiling shelves are lined with imported jars, oils and vinegars, while hams swing overhead and the deli counter groans with freshly made pasta, antipasti and exceptional cheeses. It's the perfect place to assemble a premium picnic or picky tea. Head to their Caffè Bar at the back too, should browsing work up an appetite.

19 Elm Row, EH7 4AA
valvonacrolla.co.uk

For a night of
food
& drink
VALVONA & CROLLA

39

W. ARMSTRONG & SON

Vintage gems in the historic Grassmarket

Armstrongs is one of the oldest vintage clothing emporiums in the UK, trading since 1840, and visiting is a rite of passage for anyone second-hand hunting in Edinburgh. Step inside the flagship Grassmarket store and you're met with groaning rails of kilts, military garb and theatrical pieces, but don't stop there. Push further in and that's where the real treasure hunt begins, with racks of everyday clothing spanning the decades. You'll find a mix of students piecing together last-minute outfits and locals deep in the racks searching for something unique. It's busy, chaotic and packed to the rafters, so give yourself time – the best finds rarely reveal themselves quickly. No luck hitting the vintage jackpot? There are several other branches across the city to continue the hunt.

81–83 Grassmarket, EH1 2HJ
Other locations: multiple, see website
armstrongsvintage.co.uk

L N E R
Denim Skirts

ologies but
se items are
for sale, they
part of displays
We operate a
No refund
No exchange
policy in all of our
shops thank you

40

IOLLA

Spectacular spectacles without eye-watering prices

In Scotland, if you spot someone wearing great glasses and ask where they're from, chances are the answer will be IOLLA. Founded in Glasgow in 2015, the eyewear brand quickly built a loyal following through its huge variety of designs and straightforward flat-fee pricing model, which includes lens thinning and coatings for both glasses and prescription sunglasses. The Bruntsfield showroom, the newest of several across Scotland, lets you try hundreds of frame options and lens tints, and in-store stylists guide you towards what suits. Look out for frames compatible with clip-on sunglasses, so one pair can work double duty year-round.

162–164 Bruntsfield Place, EH10 4ER
Other location: Saint James Square, EH1 3AD
iolla.com

IOLLA
OPEN
OPENING
HOURS

41
GOLDEN HARE BOOKS

Snug indie bookshop

Arguably Edinburgh's cosiest independent bookshop, this is the place to 'coorie in' (a Scots phrase meaning to nestle) on a cold day, with a log-burning stove quietly crackling through winter. Shelves are lined with bestsellers alongside niche titles, dotted with handwritten recommendations from the staff, making for a personalised browsing experience. Hidden at the back is a dedicated children's room, fully stocked and complete with tiny chairs to keep younger readers happily occupied. You'll find it on a stretch known for its independent shops, perfect for a slower afternoon of browsing.

68 St Stephen Street, EH3 5AQ
goldenharebooks.com

My Year in Paris with Gertrude Stein
Deborah Levy
Soft Core
Soft Core
Clown Town
Mick Herron

42

LIFESTORY

Scandinavian and Scottish homewares

This beautifully curated, Scandinavian design-led home and lifestyle store is at the foot of Broughton Street, one of the city's best stretches for independent shopping. Every surface is carefully considered, with Nordic pieces sitting alongside work from local makers; you'll want to take your time browsing brands such as HAY and Ferm Living. The selection strikes a balance of practical and covetable, with everyday objects elevated through sleek design. It's particularly good in the run-up to Christmas for upgraded stocking fillers – the kind you'd actually want to receive – but equally rewarding year-round if you're looking to bring something a little bit special home.

53 London Street, EH3 6LX

lifestoryshop.com

dook
dook
dook
dook
dook
dook
dook
dook
dook

43
GROW URBAN

Gardening oasis and coffee shop

Houseplant lovers and green-thumbed enthusiasts – this one's for you. Behind a handsome Georgian frontage sits grow urban, a true oasis in the city. It stocks everything the urban gardener might need, from lush greenery for compact gardens and an extensive indoor plant selection to soils, compost, tools and beautifully made pots and terrariums. Within the shop is a small cafe with tables scattered among leafy ferns and trailing vines, making it a lovely spot to pause for locally roasted coffee and cake. If you fall for something you can't carry home, UK-wide delivery means you don't have to leave it behind.

8b St Vincent Street, EH3 6SH

growurban.uk

PLANTS
grow urban.
CITY
GARDENING
grow urban.

44

ROYAL BOTANIC GARDEN EDINBURGH

Historic horticultural haven

The soaring Victorian and Georgian glasshouses are the garden's defining feature, lush with towering palms and vast lily pads and set to reopen in late 2026 after a major renovation. Beyond them, 70 acres of landscaped parkland unfold just one mile north of the city centre. Families picnic on the lawns in summer and spot ducks by the pond, while keen gardeners browse the bountiful vegetable plots supplying the Gateway Cafe. Tucked away within the Queen Mother's Memorial Garden, the Pavilion is a hidden highlight, decorated with thousands of shells and a roof made from pinecones gathered on the estate. Spring and summer bring dazzling colour, while autumn's woodland displays are just as special.

Arboretum Place, EH3 5NZ

rbge.org.uk

45

ARTHUR'S SEAT & HOLYROOD PARK

Spectacular views from an extinct volcano

A walk (never a hike in Scotland, no matter the height of the hill) up Arthur's Seat is considered a must on any Edinburgh visit. The highest of the city's seven hills, it sits just beyond the Old Town, rising to 251 metres above sea level within Holyrood Park, at the foot of the Royal Mile. Many visitors make straight for the volcano's summit, a steady climb of around an hour rewarded with stunning panoramic views at the top. But for something quieter, head instead to nearby Salisbury Crags. The views are just as impressive, while the broad plateau offers more space to wander, making it far easier to find a peaceful spot for a windy picnic without the crowds.

Queen's Drive, EH8 8HG
historicenvironment.scot/visit-a-place/places holyrood-park

46

PENTLAND HILLS

Walkers' paradise close to the city

A constant backdrop wherever you are in the city, the Pentland Hills offer a quick escape into the countryside on the outskirts of Edinburgh. This vast regional park is a haven for lovers of the outdoors, with miles of walking trails, fishing lochs and even a dry ski slope and alpine coaster. On sunny days the car parks fill quickly, but public transport links make it easy to reach popular starting points. A classic route is the Five Peaks walk from Nine Mile Burn, a roughly 10-kilometre trail that can be completed in around five hours. It takes in a string of summits with sweeping views across land and sea before finishing at The Flotterstone Inn, perfectly placed for a well-earned drink and a bowl of chips.

Flotterstone, EH26 0PP

pentlandhills.org

47

CALTON HILL

History on a hilltop

Many guides point visitors towards Arthur's Seat, the city's highest peak, but I'd argue Calton Hill is the better first stop. Set just beyond Princes Street, it offers panoramic views across Edinburgh without the lung-busting climb. At the summit, a cluster of historic monuments adds to the drama, including the never-finished National Monument (often dubbed 'Edinburgh's Disgrace'). It's a prime place to watch the sunrise or sunset over the city, with tons of space so you needn't worry about it getting too crowded. If you need a refuel, glass-fronted Cafe Calton is perfect for a coffee or light bite, with one of the best views in town.

Calton Hill, EH7 5AA
ewh.org.uk/calton-hill

DUGALD STEWART

48

WATER OF LEITH

Picturesque walk along the city's river

Stretching 20 kilometres from Balerno on the city's outskirts to The Shore in Leith, this riverside path offers one of Edinburgh's most scenic walks. Few tackle the full route, instead choosing a favourite section. The Galleries of Modern Art (no.7) are a great starting point, joining the path by Modern Two. From there, follow the river through the idyllic Dean Village and on to Stockbridge, continuing via St Mark's Park to the water's mouth at The Shore. Along the walk (which should take two hours or so), look out for Antony Gormley's standing figures (there are six) dotted throughout the river – and, if you're lucky, the occasional otter.

Damside, EH4 3BE
waterofleith.org.uk/walkway

49

PORTOBELLO BEACH

Bustling promenade and beachfront

A quick 20-minute hop on the number 26 bus from the city centre lands you at Edinburgh's most buzzy beach in the coastal Portobello suburb. This two-mile stretch of coastline combines sandy shores with a lively Victorian promenade. Most visitors gravitate to the north end of the prom, near Nobles Amusements (where many a pound has been sacrificed to the penny pushers). Here, you'll find local food favourites, with Civerinos serving chewy, well-charred pizza and Shrimp-Wreck dishing up seafood for beachside lunches and early suppers. Brave wild swimmers can warm up afterwards with coffee and cake from The Beach House.

1 Promenade, EH15 2DX

50
THE BALMORAL

Edinburgh's grande-dame station hotel

Edinburgh's most iconic hotel, this landmark of old-world glamour rises above the east end of Princes Street. Built as the city's grand railway hotel, it still greets arrivals at neighbouring Waverley Station with its towering clock, which famously runs three minutes fast to keep passengers punctual. Inside, sweeping staircases, polished marble and hushed corridors set the tone, alongside a newly renovated Sicilian-inspired luxury spa, while rooms are traditional and deeply comfortable. Dining is a serious affair here – whether a cream tea at Palm Court or the tasting menu at Number One (save room for the petit fours, wheeled to your table on a trolley).

1 Princes Street, EH2 2EQ
roccofortehotels.com/hotels-and-resorts/the-balmoral-hotel

51

GLENEAGLES TOWNHOUSE

Luxurious hotel and members club

Perthshire's iconic Gleneagles golf resort brought its signature polish to the capital when it opened an outpost here in 2022. A converted former bank in the heart of town, the hotel offers 33 elegant bedrooms, pairing maximalist design with deeply comfortable furnishings. A nod to the building's former life can be seen in the state-of-the-art gym set within the old vaults, complete with cryotherapy chambers and infrared saunas. The former banking hall houses The Spence, serving refined British dishes. The building also operates as a members' club, with co-working spaces and a busy events programme. Come summer, rooftop bar Lamplighters is one of the city's best sunset spots (exclusively open to hotel guests and Townhouse members).

39 St Andrew Square, EH2 2AD

gleneagles.com/townhouse

52

EDEN LOCKE

Colourful aparthotel in the city centre

Part aparthotel, part social hub, Eden Locke is as much about its lobby cafe and co-working space as it is the rooms upstairs. Set in a Georgian townhouse on elegant George Street, the light-filled ground floor draws a steady mix of locals, remote workers and guests, shifting gear into a relaxed wine bar by evening. You don't need a laptop to feel at home here – it's just as good for a quick coffee or a glass of something later on. Upstairs, apartments come in a range of sizes, all with kitchenettes and seating areas, offering a flexible base if you don't want to eat out for every meal. Interiors pair clean Scandi lines with playful pops of colour.

127 George Street, EH2 4JN
lockeliving.com/en/edinburgh/eden-locke

53

SANDY BELL'S

A local folk music institution

Step into Sandy Bell's and you'll almost always be met with live music, whether it's a solo guitarist working through a new tune or a group of local folk musicians jamming together – with animated crowd participation as the night goes on. Don't expect set times or line-ups here; instead, it feels like you've stumbled into a session already in full swing, usually gathered in the small musicians' nook at the back. Up front, the bar pours a solid range of local draught beers, cask ales and a generous selection of malt whiskies. It's the perfect place to hunker down by the fire after a chilly walk across the nearby Meadows.

25 Forrest Road, EH1 2QH

sandybells.com

FORREST HILL
WHISKY
Sandy Bell's
MERCHANTS
Sandy Bell's
Sandy Bell's
WORLD RENOWNED FOLK BAR
25
Sandy Bell's
WHISKY MERCHANTS
WORLD RENOWNED FOLK BAR
Sandy Bell's
MERCHANTS

54

SMITH & GERTRUDE

Cosy wine and charcuterie spot

Time has a habit of slipping away at this welcoming Stockbridge wine bar, where a single glass turns into a whole afternoon spent with friends. You can pick from their wide-ranging list of old and new world vintages or opt for a wine flight to try something new (the cheese pairing for each glass is well worth adding on). The food offering is simple, centred around cheese and charcuterie boards, but the toasties have become something of a house signature. If you find a favourite wine, many bottles from the cellar are available to take home too.

26 Hamilton Place, EH3 5AU

Other location: 254 Portobello High Street, EH15 2AT

smithandgertrude.com

EDINBURGH
SMITH &
GERTRUDE
WINE. CHEESE. COMPANY.

55

SPRY

The city's coolest wine bar

Every city worth its salt has a natural wine bar where the cool crowd gathers, and Spry is Edinburgh's answer. The interior is pared back, with white walls and mid-century seating letting the bottle-lined shelves do the talking. Despite the refined, chic look, the atmosphere is relaxed and welcoming, with staff always happy to guide you towards something you'll love. Wine is the main focus, as you'd expect, but there's a tight food menu of small plates for lunch and dinner too. Come the Edinburgh summer, the outdoor bench is the place to be seen on a sunny weekend, glass in hand.

1 Haddington Place, EH7 4AE

sprywines.co.uk

TIERRA!
OSARELLA

Tillingham
Field Blend
Two
2021
COWBOYS
MOUNTAIN
PEOPLE WINE
UN
ÉTÉ GREC
NESTAREC
Pink
ČTYRY
VALLI ROSSO
matilde
PÀCINA
VALLI ROSA

56
NEWBARNS BREWERY

Local brewery taproom in Leith

Newbarns is about a mile and a half out of the city centre – a 10-minute hop by taxi or tram, or a half-hour stroll along Leith Walk if you want to stretch your legs. Down a side street off the bottom of Leith Walk, it feels like a bit of a find. It's a brewery that's serious about beer, but the atmosphere is anything but – more like a relaxed, down-to-earth pub that just happens to have tanks bubbling away next door. Inside, it's all eclectic vintage furniture, with a well-used dartboard and a steady stream of locals settling in for a pint. Weekend food pop-ups often showcase emerging street food vendors, meaning you'll likely stumble across something you won't find elsewhere in the city, alongside their popular weekly pub quiz (free to enter).

13 Jane Street, EH6 5HE
newbarnsbrewery.com

newbarns

11
IPA

NEWBARNS
BREWERY

57

HEY PALU

Playful Italian cocktail bar

Enter this Italian cocktail bar and you'll feel instantly at home, with a little glass of peanuts plonked down as soon as you order. Hey Palu may not take itself too seriously, but it takes its drinks very seriously indeed. Negronis are the headline act – stick with the classic or order a flight to sample inventive twists. The dirty martini with a blue cheese-stuffed olive is exceptional, and even playful touches, like a Paper Plane served with DIY origami, are executed properly. It's just a really great place to settle in for a very good drink.

49 Bread Street, EH3 9AH

heypalu.com

GORDAL PICANTE
Perelló

58

THE LAST WORD

Familiar cocktail bar with wide whisky selection

Descending the stairs of a Stockbridge basement, this low-lit cocktail bar feels like a secret – and one you should know. Inside, dark wood tables and plush leather seating create an intimate, date-night atmosphere. Slightly removed from the city centre hubbub, it attracts a loyal local crowd rather than passing tourists. The cocktail list feels creative without veering towards gimmicky, and if whisky is on your Edinburgh agenda, this is a strong place to begin. With over 100 bottles behind the bar, including a rotating selection poured at cost price, you can taste something special without overspending. Reservations are wise at weekends.

44 St Stephen Street, EH3 5AL
lastwordsaloon.com

IMAGE CREDITS

Page 2 © Dapples Photography; Page 4 © Mike Newbry / Unsplash; Page 6 © Tina Leahy; Page 7 © Colin Meg; Page 8 © Kieran Dunning; Page 9 © Darcie Maher; Page 10 © Murray Orr; The Edinburgh Festival Fringe © Roberto Ricciuti / Getty Images; Edinburgh Castle first image © Guven Ozdemir / Getty Images, second image © Yujie Chen / Getty Images; Jupiter Artland first image © PA Images / Alamy, second and third image © Allan Pollok-Morris; National Galleries of Scotland, first image © Daisy Wingate-Saul, second image © Dapples Photography; Fruitmarket Gallery first image: Pardes, 2022. Installation view Fruitmarket Warehouse. Courtesy the artist. Photo © Tom Nolan. Second image: Karla Black sculptures (2001–2021) details for a retrospective, installation view Fruitmarket 2021. Photo © Ruth Clark. Third image: Poor Things, installation view Fruitmarket 2023. Photo © Tom Nolan; Dominion Cinema © Richard Newton / Alamy; Surgeons' Hall Museum © Lucy Thomas / Alamy; Port of Leith Distillery © Murray Orr; Santu Roastery © Murray Orr; Fortitude Coffee © Alix McIntosh; Barry Fish © Murray Orr; Stockbridge Eating House © Dani Campbell; Pomelo © Sound Bite PR; The Gilded Saloon © The Gilded Saloon; Nishiki © Sound Bite PR; The Palmerston first image © James Porteous, second image © Tina Leahy; Norah © Christina Leahy; Mother India's Cafe © Murray Orr; Alby's © Murray Orr; Little Capo © Stephen Lister; The Free Company © Masters & Masters; Ardfern first image © Gabrielle Roberts, second and third image © AwAye Media; Dogstar © Nathan Hinze; Montrose © Abi Radford; Sotto © Tina Leahy; LYLA © Murray Orr; Ante first and second image © Christina Leahy, third image © Paris Wilson; Lannan Bakery first image © Darcie Mahar, second image © ZAC and ZAC; skout © Gemma Christina McNaughton; treen © Murray Orr; Frontiers Man © Frontiers; Jorum Studio © Cro & Kow; TBCo © Murray Orr; Edinburgh Mercantile © Kieran Dunning; Valvona & Crolla © Krzysztof Globisz; W. Armstrong & Son Vintage © Murray Orr; IOLLA © Cameron Malcolm; Golden Hare Books © Julia König; Lifestory © Simon Hird; grow urban © Murray Orr; Royal Botanic Gardens Edinburgh first image © Raquel Arocena Torres / Getty Images, second image © Alisha Bube / Getty Images, third image © David C Tomlinson / Getty Images; Arthur's Seat & Holyrood Park first image © Kurt Pacaud / Getty Images, second image © NurPhoto / Getty Images; Pentland Hills first image © Ismael Garzon / Getty Images, second image © joannatkaczuk / Getty Images; Calton Hill first image © Yassine AMRI / Getty Images, second image © ewg3D / Getty Images; Water of Leith © Serts / Getty Images; Portobello Beach © Felix Mizioznikov / Alamy; The Balmoral © The Balmoral, a Rocco Forte hotel; Gleneagles Townhouse © Gleneagles Townhouse; Eden Locke © Nicholas Worley; Sandy Bells © Michelle Bailey / Alamy; Smith & Gertrude © Amelia & Christian Masters; Spry first image © Siobhan Nevada, second image © Paris Wilson, third image © Siobhan Nevada; Newbarns Brewery © Murray Orr; Hey Palu first image © Gabrielle Roberts, second and third image © Sam Christie / AwAye Media; The Last Word © Murray Orr.

An Opinionated Guide to Edinburgh
First edition, first printing

Published in 2026 by Hoxton Mini Press, London.

Text by Pippa Perriam
Editing by Gaynor Sermon
Production design by Dom Grant
Production control by David Brimble
Proofreading by Emma Seckel
Additional editorial support by Kate Overy & Olivia Kumar

With thanks to Matthew Young for initial series design.

Please note: we recommend checking the websites listed for each entry before you visit for the latest information on price, opening times and pre-booking requirements.

Thank you to all of the individuals and institutions who have provided images and arranged permissions. While every effort has been made to trace the present copyright holders we apologise in advance for any unintentional omission or error, and would be pleased to insert the appropriate acknowledgement in any subsequent edition.

A CIP catalogue record for this book is available from the British Library.

ISBN: 978-1-917719-40-7

Printed and bound by OZGraf, Poland

Manufacturer: Hoxton Mini Press, 104 Northside Studios, 16–29 Andrews Road, London E8 4QF, UK
www.hoxtonminipress.com

Represented by: Authorised Rep Compliance Ltd., Ground Floor, 71 Lower Baggot Street, Dublin D02 P593, Ireland
www.arccompliance.com

Hoxton Mini Press is an environmentally conscious publisher, committed to offsetting our carbon footprint. This book is 100 per cent carbon compensated, with offset purchased from Stand For Trees.

Every time you order from our website, we plant a tree: www.hoxtonminipress.com

FSC www.fsc.org
MIX
Paper | Supporting responsible forestry
FSC® C163799

Selected opinionated guides in the series:

For more go to www.hoxtonminipress.com

INDEX